TABLE OF CONTENTS

MW00954712

About the Book:
This book is comprised of more than two dozen famous themes by Mozart which are provided in a comfortable range and key for the student player. Dynamics, articulations and phrase markings etc. are intentionally omitted but may be added by the teacher as deemed appropriate for each student.

DEH VENI, NON TARDAR

from *The Marriage of Figaro*

Andante

DOVE SONO
from *The Marriage of Figaro*

Andantino

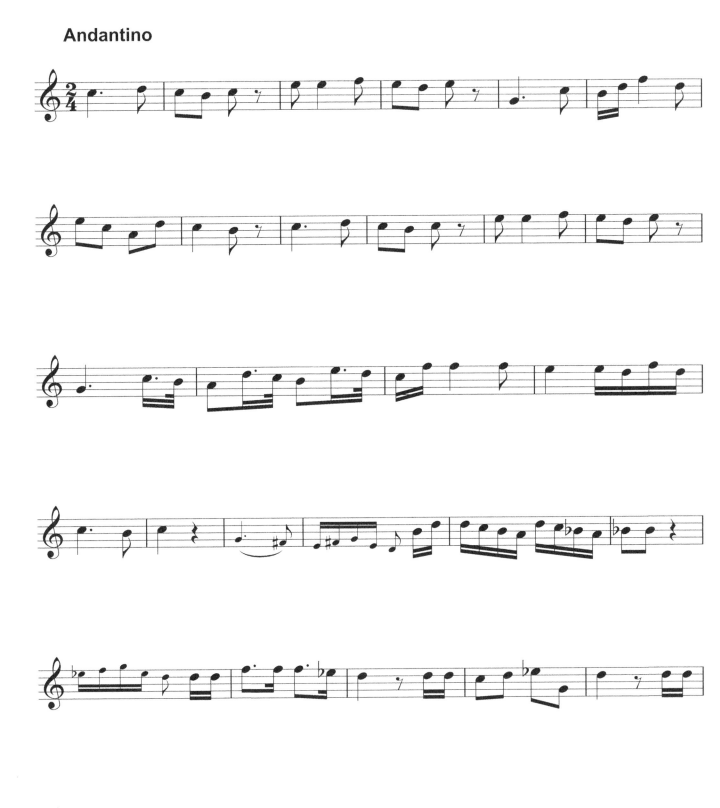

EINE KLEINE NACHTMUSIK K. 525

First Movement Theme

Allegro

8

Second Movement Theme

Andante

Third Movement Theme (Minuet)

Allegretto

Fourth Movement Theme

Allegro

GERMAN DANCE

Stately

HORN CONCERTO IN Eb MAJOR K. 447
Third Movement Theme

O ISIS UND OSIRIS

from *The Magic Flute*

Adagio

MINUET IN F

Moderato

MINUET IN G

Moderato

NON PIU ANDRAI

from *The Marriage of Figaro*

Vivace

NON SO PIU
from *The Marriage of Figaro*

Allegro vivace

D.C. al Fine

OVERTURE TO DON GIOVANNI

Molto allegro

OVERTURE TO THE MAGIC FLUTE

Adagio

OVERTURE TO THE MARRIAGE OF FIGARO

Allegro

Presto

PIANO CONCERTO IN C MAJOR K. 467

First Movement Theme

PIANO CONCERTO IN C MAJOR K. 467

Second Movement Theme

SONATA IN A MAJOR K. 331

Andante grazioso

PORGI, AMOR

from *The Marriage of Figaro*

Larghetto

Wolfgang Amadeus Mozart

Wolfgang Amadeus Mozart (1756 - 1791) was a child prodigy. By age five he could play the violin and piano and at 17 he played for the King.

He composed more than 600 works and is among the most famous composers of all time.

SE VUOL BALLARE

from *The Marriage of Figaro*

Allegretto

SYMPHONY NO. 39 IN E♭ MAJOR K. 543

Third Movement Theme

Allegretto

SYMPHONY NO. 40 IN G MINOR K. 550

First Movement Theme

Molto Allegro

Fourth Movement Theme

Allegro assai

Wolfgang Amadeus Mozart
1756 - 1791

Fine

Trio

D.C. Minuet

VIOLIN CONCERTO IN G K. 216

First Movement Theme

Allegro

VOI, CHE SAPETE

from *The Marriage of Figaro*

Andante con moto

Made in the USA
Monee, IL
03 April 2021